Our First Year

Sketches from an Alpine Village

Allen E. Rizzi

Dedication

To my wife Rachel for her constant love and willingness to share a dream together.

t'amo sempre!

Preface

The South Tirol is an area that spreads south from the Austrian Alps into the northern most expanses of Italy. The area is typified by a Germanic heritage uniquely altered in the various valleys that dot the terrain. It is in these valleys, each unique in its language, history and customs, that one finds the true heart of the South Tirol. One of these valleys that lie on the Southern flank of the Tirol is my ancestral home, the Val di Non.

In 1913, my father was born in the tiny village of Tret in the valley's upper most reaches. It is a place of which I knew nothing until I was myself over fifty years old. Several vacation trips to the area provided the impetus for my wife and me moving here to live permanently in 2003. It was a large decision, prompted in part by our curiosity and hunger for a small place in the world where we really believed we belonged.

The Val di Non is a valley, more accurately a region of Northern Italy, flanked by the Dolomites to the east, the Ortler Alps to the north and bound by a band of magnificent mountains, rich green forests and alpine lakes. Being part of lower Austria until 1918, the area's culture is a breed of Austrian, Tirolean, Italian and German with remnants of the previous Roman, Latin, and French influences. The Val di Non lies almost entirely within the province of Trento in the Trentino region and borders its sister province, Bolzano in the Alto-Adige region. While the Alto-Adige retains an official dual language status incorporating both German and Italian, Trentino's tongue is a mix of Italian, some German and a variety of local Italian dialects that are spoken in its various valleys. Both Bolzano and Trento are autonomous provinces of Italy and therefore retain much of their independent character that has been born of hundreds of years of struggle, foreign invasions and changes of governments and languages.

An ancient land full of old castles, old villages and old customs, the Val di Non is the largest valley in the Trento province and home to a booming, modern agricultural economy based on apple production. The paradox of old and new may be seen at every turn. The church bells still sound on the hour as you shop for a new computer in Cavareno. Across the valley in Cloz, one can absorb the sweet aroma of ripening apples in September while gazing at Roman artifacts on display that that date from the first century. In the tiny village of Senale, the hay is still harvested with a hand held scythe while next to the fields there stands a newly created nature preserve with its small man made pond. The land here is rich. The soil produces the new economy, a unique history that is complex and a life that is simple.

The valley is roughly divided into three parts. The upper valley, known as the *Alta Val di Non*, comprises an area that stretches from the village of Senale to the town of Fondo and incorporates a crescent of other small villages. The Noce River dissects the valley, creating the lower portion with the valley's chief city, Cles. Then there is the so-called *Terza Sponda*, (Third Bank), the portion of the *Alta Val di Non* that is dissected by and east of the Novella stream.

Each has its own unique character that has been molded throughout thousands of years of history. However, the common threads that bind the valley and its people together have always been God, family and the land.
Tret is a very small village and in actuality a *frazione* (administrative district) of the larger village of Fondo, some 8 kilometers

to the South. The population here is officially 280, including me and my wife. The people who live here tend to be older, over 75 years on average. The official language is Nones; a complicated dialect based on vulgar Latin with influences of German and Italian.

Tret was written about extensively in the famous book, *The Hidden Frontier (1974, John W. Cole and Eric R. Wolf)*, which dealt academically with the differences between Italian speaking Tret and its German speaking neighboring village of San Felice. It is a valuable source for understanding the cultural differences found here. This book, by contrast, endeavors to bring the village of Tret and its surroundings to life with fact, personalities and a little humor.

My first book, *Coming Home – An Anthology of Heritage*, explains the reasons behind our decision to move to Tret, Italy. My wife and I moved to Tret permanently on May 21, 2003. This book moves forward from the first and attempts to sketch this beautiful land in several short stories in order to give the reader a first-hand glimpse of our experiences with Tret, its surroundings and its people. The stories are told using real people and real places; to do otherwise would be dishonest and detract from the purpose. This book offers the reader brief sketches of the life and people here in the Italian Alps as seen through the eyes of a new immigrant from America.

Tret has been my home and the very heart of my existence for over ten years. Living here represents a dream fulfilled but it has not been without its dark moments of insecurity. The road to Tret was indeed very long for me and my wife, fraught with obstacles and a long list of adjustments. It has, in the end, been a very worthwhile experience which has enriched our lives immeasurably.

The Sketches

Crossroads in the Sky

For some strange reason, I have always lived where planes crisscross the sky above me every day. It was true fifty years ago when I lived as a child near Los Angeles in the small town of San Fernando, California. This then rural enclave of greater Los Angeles was wide open with wonder five decades ago. As a youngster I often mused at where life would take me. Every day, I would gaze upward to see the small planes that landed at our nearby municipal airport. Occasionally, larger planes would pass overhead with thunderous roar as they headed for the Los Angeles International Airport some twenty-five miles south of our home. The years changed many things, but not the odd occurrence of living beneath airplanes and their tracks in the sky. By luck or chance, I always found myself in a home directly underneath crossroads in the sky.

Later as a young man, I again looked up and sure enough those planes were there. This time the location was in Granada Hills, California and I was already married with a child on the way. The planes had become larger and less noisy as they passed overhead. But there in the heavens they were always a part of my everyday life. As I watched my son grow too quickly from a baby to a young man, the one constant in my life seemed to be that I lived beneath those connecting white lines in the sky. Gradually, I began to see this phenomenon as a comforting bellwether of my existence. As the hum of single engine two-seater planes gave way to the white vapor trails seven miles above me, I was always reassured by their presence and took them to be signs of some significance and comfort. They seemed to mark the spot below them where I should be, in a greater sense, where I should dwell. So despite the small failures in my life, I always felt somehow right in my endeavors and reassured of their outcome wherever I lived. These signs in the skies consoled my spirit and moved me forever onward.

After marrying a second time, I moved to the rural suburbs of Agoura Hills in Southern California and again I found it reassuring to see those white tails in the blue above, a reminder that I was indeed in my right spot on this planet. I had made the right decisions and there were signs in the heavens to proclaim it so. Doubts were cast aside and I moved on with confidence. Some years later found me living on the Oregon coast and even here the small planes from the local Gold Beach municipal airport and their larger cousins were in the skies over my home daily to state without question that I was again in my proper place. The skies had marked the way. The place was always proper although the precise spot, in the physical sense, had moved many times across the American landscape.

Years moved ahead in quick succession and so did my choices for where to live. Constantly, I was in search for a quieter place in this world; one in which I could find the solace of peace. Oregon was a calm place that embodied a pioneer spirit, which I enjoyed. I arrived in Eugene, Oregon one cold rainy morning and to my delight, one of the first things I heard was a jet plane overhead in the clouds. Later, I learned that Eugene had a small airport with connecting flights to the whole world. I settled there for nearly twenty years. In all of that time, I lived in two homes; both were directly underneath the great North-South flight paths of the major West Coast airports. I would somewhat jokingly exhort, "We are under the wings again!" With that light-hearted statement, life always felt settled and soothed.

I would gaze upward on clear days and watch as these planes took eager passengers south to the warm, tropical shores of Mexico or North to connect with waiting planes to exciting destinations in the Far East or Europe. I wondered at their destinations and wondered too at where their vapor trails might point me next. I lived my life calmly and dreamed my dreams with assurance, but always with one eye above me in the hope that I would see something more there; perhaps a greater sign, an oracle of sorts in the shades between the blue and the white streaks.

I have come to believe that there are no epiphanies in life but only a series of recognitions of what was to be despite our best efforts. In 1997, I made my first trip to

Europe with the hope of discovering a bit of what made me and to tap the roots of my ancestry. In the process, I became enchanted with the alpine valley in Italy where my father had been born just before World War I. This valley, the Val di Non, was the cradle of my family's history and I felt immediately at home. After several more vacation trips with my wife at my side, I began to realize that this is where I needed to be next in this life. After some deliberation, we purchased a home in the tiny village of Tret. Then we began to make the tough and often painful decisions that were necessary to move to our new home in the Italian Alps. Furniture was sold, favorite old books given away and a lot of effort and money was spent. Old friendships were shaken to test their resolve and two parents did not live to see the fruits of our decisions. In the end, even our beloved cat and dog both died before we were able to transform our plan into reality. However, in the end there was a familiar airplane waiting at the Eugene airport. Once aboard I could not help but wonder at those people in the tiny Oregon houses below us and how that some of them might be gazing upward as we departed for a new life. Were there others like me? Would they look up and see the plane? Would they have their own dreams to dream? Would I help mark their spot below?

We dreamed our dreams and now we are busy living them. Our home is high in the Dolomite Mountains and the planes overhead look so much closer now. And so much closer too are the heavens in which they travel lightly like goose down blown by a soft breeze. I watch them often but now with a different perspective. They have, after all, delivered me to what I believe is my proper destination. And so I sit here this morning, first gazing at the valley below me in its rich shades of green and fullness rimmed in snow and beauty. I hear the small hum overhead as I sip my espresso deliberately. I gaze upward, as I have thousands of times before, to see two distinct streaks of white behind the silver bullet high in the sky. I draw a sigh and with a mother's comfort I am reminded that I am once again at home beneath the crossroads in the sky.

The Alimentari

The front of the old building is plain and it looks like what one might expect in any small village in Northern Italy. The stucco is accented by dark wood trim and there are the small signs that announce that this place is an *alimentari* or small general store where foodstuffs may be purchased. And of course, there are geraniums neatly arranged in flower boxes supported by the balcony's iron fence. It is an ordinary building in an ordinary village named Tret.

However, like many things in this part of the world, looks are often deceiving in that they hide the subtle important shades of a rich history. What is now simply a storefront with rented rooms above was once interwoven in the beginnings of my family's history. The history is complex, even a bit confusing, but in the end it serves as a full explanation of who I am.

I first saw this building during my initial trip to Italy in 1997. I was indeed excited to see it as my father was born there in 1913 in a small room in the upper right side of the building's front, which faces the small street, *Via Principale*. I took several photos of the building and met the current owner. Thus began my exploration of this special place. The building's current owner is Nella Pittino, a widow who lives with her daughter Antonella. Together they operate Tret's only small market. People come and go all day long for items that range from the simple bread and eggs to postcards and stamps to propane gas tanks to feed their stoves. It is a central meeting spot in this small part of the world and the building itself has been important here for hundreds of years.

Before the building was an *alimentari* under the ownership of the Pittino family, it served as a post office, *albergo* (hotel) and small store under the ownership of one of the many Bertagnolli families of Tret. This particular Bertagnolli family was comprised of Emmanuele Bertagnolli and his wife Armida Flor. Armida was my father's aunt and so the recent history began.

Armida and Emmanuele Bertagnolli were strong people who had made their lives and fortunes in America as emigrants in the late 1890's. They returned to their native Tret with some amount of money and purchased the building from the Segna family who had operated small businesses there for some years. Armida and Emmanule, or *Zia Nani* and *Zio Mani* as they were called by local residents, began several business there in the early 1900's. These included Tret's first post office and the village's only hotel and restaurant. Life was good in those early years of the last century and their businesses flourished. They extended their holdings in and around Tret to include several pieces of land, one of which was a swampy   field far above Tret that was destined to become Lake Tret. However, in the earlier days of the 1900's, this Bertagnolli family was content to operate their hotel and restaurant and enjoy the simple pleasures that this village still offers.

Armida's sister Anna had also gone to the United States as an emigrant in 1896. There she married my grandfather Eugenio Rizzi in Rock Springs, Wyoming. Like her sister, she enjoyed success and relative wealth in America and began raising a family while her husband continued to parlay his money into larger and more lucrative business holdings. Anna's life was a true reflection of the *American Dream* until 1912. In this year her husband Eugenio Rizzi fell through the ice on a stream while rounding-up sheep on his Wyoming ranch. Although he recovered, this accident left his health in jeopardy and the entire family moved back to what was then Austria where they lived in houses they had purchased in nearby Merano. Later in the year, the couple visited Armida and Emmanule in Tret at the Bertagnolli house where Eugenio fell victim to a heart attack. He died there at the kitchen table at the age of 38.

This was of course a shock to Eugenio's wife Anna. Even worse, Anna was now two months pregnant with my father and did not have a family of her own to help her through the birth process. So ironically, Anna went to Tret to live with her sister and give birth to her last child, my father Eugenio Rizzi. On a cold April 1 in 1913, my father was born in a tiny room on the second floor of the Bertagnolli Albergo. He was named Eugenio for his late father. The joy of the new child's arrival was soon crushed by the death of Anna's only daughter, Rosalia. Ironically, she also died from heart disease in the house that is now the alimentari, at age 14. Life can be and certainly was cruel.

My father spent his early youth traveling between Tret, Merano and Rock Springs, Wyoming in the United States. He remembered vividly the weekly treks from Tret to Merano that comprised 6 hours of steady walking. When he was only two years old, he enjoyed this trip perched in a rucksack atop his brother Rinaldo's back. Later, he made the trip in earnest and learned what a good walk was really all about. He remembered all of his long life eating snails during Tret's long winters because of the family's thriftiness. He remembered the smell of the stalls and cows that were below his bedroom window. Most of all, he remembered the good lessons that were taught him here in Tret and later applied these to become the most excellent of husbands and fathers.

The *alimentari* is today the center of all things in this tiny village. On any given day, you may find a great number of Tret's inhabitants going in and out of this busy little store. Here a person can buy near all of life's necessities and catch-up on local news and gossip. Such stores do not exist any longer in the United States to any great degree. Here, they are most needed and most welcomed in any small community. It has a special significance to me. When I pass its stone walls, neatly covered in white stucco, I think back to a century before and smile at the irony that I am now walking the same cobble stone streets that my grandparents once walked.

I am honored to be a part of this small community. Its people have welcomed me and my wife as their children and they have accepted us both for who we are. They have been generous in their kindness, the sharing of their knowledge and their everyday help.

We will always be grateful to all of Tret's other 278 residents.

Buildings are of stone and they do not hear the sounds of the church bells ringing the years in and out. They stand as mute sentinels guarding their towns and all of their secrets. If you ever come here to Tret you may wonder a bit about the buildings here. They are very old, many dating to the 1600s and they have very old stories. They all hold well their secrets of hundreds of years of history. Each stone here has its own story. With some of these stones, you will find a little history and if you press your ear close to some of them, they will reveal their secrets. Of this I can say for certain.

Le Lapidi

Stone is hard but it is not forever. Life is hard but not forever. These two absolutes are ever present here in my new valley, my new home.

Years ago, I was told of the grave markers of my grandfather and of my aunt and how they occupy an unusual place in the town of my ancestors. The story was old and my memory not too good, so I forgot most of what I had been told as a child. Children are, after-all, concerned with the living and not the dead. My curiosity was aroused when I was in my early twenties. My parents made their only trip to Europe in 1972 and returned home with a variety of grainy photographs. One of them was of my grandfather's grave marker, or *lapide*. The old stone was cut deeply to reveal a full-face portrait of my grandfather in real life dimensions. As I viewed this photograph for the first time, I was immediately struck by the similarity between my grandfather and myself. In my youth, I appeared as his twin

15

brother. I often mused, in fact, that the similarity often bothered my father a bit in the sense that he had never met his own father and I was a constant reminder of this sad facet of the past. In fact, at age 26 this was the impetus for my changing the way I parted my hair.

On my first visit to Italy in 1997, one of my priorities was to find this grave marker and see it for myself. We drove to the ancestral home of my family, the small village of Cloz located under Mt. Ozol in the Val di Non. There, on the left side of Cloz's main church, St. Stefano, we found the old grave marker just as it had been described. It was a bit bruised by time and partly covered in old ivy, but appeared overall in good condition.

UNA PRECE
A
EUGENIO RIZZI
CHE NELLA VERDE ETA
DI SOLI 38 ANNI
LI 11-IX 1912
FU RAPITO ALL'AFFETTO
DE SUOI CARI

L'ADDOLORATA MOGLIE
ED I FIGLI
RICONOSCENTI

The St. Stefano church in Cloz had been
rebuilt several times in the past century.
During one of these renovations in 1933, the
cemetery had been moved from its position
in the courtyard of the church to a larger
space further down the hill and across the
main road. However, about thirty-six of the
old grave markers were left and later moved
to a wall at the left side of the church as sort
of a monument to the community's past.
Included in this group of old gravestones
were those of my grandfather Eugenio
Stefano Rizzi and my aunt Rosalia Rizzi.

They are now part of an historical monument administered by the Province of Trento and the Catholic Archdiocese of Trento.

Eugenio, my grandfather, had died tragically as a young man of 38 years at the home of his sister-in-law at Tret, the victim of a heart attack. He was later transported for burial to Cloz, his native town. This is the custom here and it is said that *you always return home to be buried.* My grandfather indeed went home to Cloz in the end. His life had been hard and it was not forever. The letters that tell of his death are cut deep in the stone but they are beginning to fade with time:

"Una prece a Eugenio Rizzi.... che nella verde eta' di soli 38 anni .... Li ii-ix-1912 fu rapito all affetto de suoi cari .... l'addolorata moglie ed I figli riconoscenti."

On this same trip, we noticed that the gravestone for my aunt Rosalia was in bad repair. When it had been constructed, there was a glass dome that covered a large photograph printed on plain paper. The wisdom of this original construction has always escaped me; perhaps the reason can be found in the fact that my aunt died at age 14 within months of my grandfather and my grandmother set about to create a grave marker with great dignity. Perhaps she failed in the end in the execution of this work as sorrow filled her life. We eventually learned that the glass dome had been destroyed 90 years before, the victim of a bullet during World War I. Other bullet strikes marked the stone as well. Since all of my remaining family left Europe for good shortly after the war, the grave marker had never been repaired and stood empty, literally without a face.

We returned two years later to repair my aunt's *lapide*, a formidable task in these parts. First, I had to locate the local expert in grave markers, one Adolfo Menghini from the neighboring village of Brez. Then, I had to explain what I wanted done in the way of work. It seemed rather bizarre to this man that I would appear from nowhere and want a work of this magnitude performed. Ignorant of the local dialect, I sketched my design in the sand in the back of his workshop and explained to his son what needed to be done. A circular ceramic photograph, measuring over a foot in diameter, had to be made in Bologna from a 90 year-old photograph and then transported to Cloz and finally placed into the cavity where the glass dome once stood proud. In all, the work took several months to accomplish. Even the words chiseled into the stone almost a hundred years ago were once again restored: *"A fianco del padre, qui giace Rosalia Rizzi alla bell'anima pace."*

Stone is not forever, but I attempted to make it so for another hundred years. The small memorial stands today as a polite reminder of a gentle little girl whom I never met. When I look deeply into her worried little eyes, I wish I had met her. I hope to meet her someday in the end.

I return often to the site of these two grave markers. They give me strength when I am feeling weakened by life's bruising blows. They remind me of my past and make me proud. They speak to me in whispered tones, to reassure me of my path, that it is true. These old bits of stone, they seem as though they guide me and that they are my compass. Above all, I am always left wishing that I could have known these two people and that they could have known me. That I am now here among them, where they once walked, loved and cried, is at the same time an immense irony and a thing of extreme beauty to my soul.

Stone is hard but it is not forever. Life is hard but not forever. These two absolutes are ever present here in my new valley, my new home.

Il Lago: Oggi e Una Volta

There is a small *lago* (lake) in the woods above the village of Tret. Today, it is a popular tourist destination for the myriad of German and Italian tourists who visit its shore every year. It is a very pretty place, high in the mountains with pleasant views of the surrounding peaks. It is also home to a large part of local history, of which I am privileged to be a part of.

Before the turn of the century (yes, the other turn of the century), there sat in the cold forest above the village a *palu*, a sort of a swampy low lying area that collected the snow runoff in the Spring. This same small depression, like a shallow bowl, was also used as a *prato* or meadow in the Summer months. The area had been used much in the same way for hundreds of years. A seasonal creek, the Vier, made its way down the steep mountain, stopping in this shallow depression before rushing down to the village of Tret. There the water was used for drinking and irrigation.

In the early 1920's, a native of the village, Emmanuele Bertagnolli, bought the land after returning from America with a modest bit of money in hand. Then in 1921 and 1922, he built a low earthen dam and the lake was born. At the official benediction of the lake in 1922 (yes, we bless the lakes here too), the lake took its official name, *Lago Santa Maria*. The local priest blessed the lake while on its waters aboard a small boat. Over the years, the small body of water also became to be known as Lake Tret and Lake San Felice, depending on which of the two villages you were from.

I come into this story in an odd way. Emmanuele Bertagnolli's wife was Armida Flor, the sister of my grandmother. Both girls were born in the village of Brez which is further down the valley in an area known today as the "terza sponda" (third bank). Armida married a man from Tret and my grandmother married my grandfather who was from Cloz, a village close to Brez. As I have already recounted, my grandfather died before my father was born. Left alone and expecting her last child, my grandmother came to Tret to live with her sister and have the baby. This is the short explanation of why a Rizzi was born in Tret. The first and the last were my father. This is also why I have so many distant cousins in the village of Tret. After my father was born, he remained in Tret and nearby Merano until about the age of five, returning in later years for vacations and small trips.

The new lake became the center of village life in the early part of the 1900's. Emmanuele Bertagnolli and his wife built a *rifugio* or small mountain hut on the banks of the lake near the dam and it was here that many a party was held. The *rifugio* also served food and drink on a regular basis and drew in both the local trade and also that of the tourists visiting the area. My father remembered spending many an afternoon at the *rifugio* and playing on the rocky outcrops behind it as his mother helped her sister prepare food. The menu in those days was richly varied but always included trout. Interestingly, the first trout were brought to the lake in its early days by Emmanuele and his brothers by horseback from Lago di

Garda which lies some 50 miles to the south. Emmanuele Bertagnolli was an enterprising man and soon after the completion of the dam, one could rent a *barca* (boat) for a Sunday afternoon on the water. The boats completed the tranquil setting above the village. All that remains of these early days is a small collection of old photos that show what life was like in the 1920s and 1930s. The men on the boats all wore their Sunday suits and ties while the women, for the most part, were arrayed in their finest clothes and fancy hats.

I have sat and marveled at these old photos many an evening and wondered what it was like during the early days of the lake. Of course I cannot say for sure, but judging by the expressions on the faces of these Sunday crowds, I can say that life was beautiful then and a thing to be enjoyed by the whole family. Life was simple, as were the meals, the boats and the lake itself. The memories endure as mere flickers of light from the past when the stories have ceased to be told and time moves us steadily and forcefully forward. The old photos, however shoddy and worn, tell the true tale of the past and for this I am thankful.

The lake has seen many changes since its inception. It has become known by many names. The official name of the lake is Lago di Santa Maria. However, it has also been known through the years as Lago di Tret, Saint Felix See (Lake of San Felice) and Lago di Salomp (named for the mountain on which the lake is situated). While the name has changed over time, so has the lake itself. Once the center of social life in the village of Tret, the lake has now become mainly an attraction for tourists. Much of the local population is too elderly to endure the very steep walk of about an hour. The road to the lake is now restricted for use only by those with property near its shores and in the surrounding mountains; it is closed to the general public.

The old *rifugio* that was built by the Bertagnolli family was destroyed by fire in the late 1960's and never rebuilt. There is a new *rifugio*, The Waldruhe, on the opposite shore near the point where the small stream feeds the lake. The lake, once owned by individuals, is now owned officially by the Province of Bolzano and maintained for minimal recreation (no boats are allowed) and for a source of irrigation water for the village of Tret. Sadly, the physical appearance of the lake has also changed a bit. From the lake's earliest days there stood on a small island in the center of the lake a larch tree. Over the years this tree grew to great proportions and became a local landmark of sorts. Then in the late 1990's, a lightning strike brought down the tree and decades of memories.

Today the lake is visited regularly by people in all four seasons. The Summer sees the heaviest volume of tourists, many from Germany, Austria and the Netherlands. It has become a "must see" destination on the tourist itinerary. After September, the crowds thin out considerably but the lake is still visited by many people each week. The lake is also popular in the Winter for ice skaters and cross country skiers. There is also a local group of men (and one woman) who visit the lake around 5 a.m. each day in the Winter to bathe nude in the frigid after cutting a hole in the ice.

I have visited the lake in all of its seasons for all of its reasons. It is the place to which I walked to ponder the future as my mother lay dying in a hospital 6,000 miles away; it is where I caught my first fish in Italy; it is where I have gone on sunny Winter days to hear the sounds of nothing; it is where I have gone to eat, to think and to pray. This lake, Lago di Tret, has been my companion and I have been hers. We understand each other, I think.

La Veneta, Il Gustavo

There are traces of every family throughout the world. They are like illusive footsteps that seem to disappear into the sand of our society. Some have been left purposefully by the family and others have been deposited by the circumstances of time. In my family, both hold true.

Years before I first set foot in the city of Merano, I heard stories from my father about several houses that my grandmother owned in this city. One was described to me as being in the center of this small city while the other was described as being a *villa*, located on the outskirts of Merano. Over the years, I had not given the subject much thought. However, after our first visit to Merano in 1997 I became curious as to where exactly these houses were located. And so began the odyssey of old house hunting.

Merano lies at the juncture of three valleys at the base of the Palade Road which runs from Tret to the Adige valley. The first house was easy to find. It is located in the center of Merano's quiet tree lined streets on a lane known as the Kloistersteig, Via Monastero in Italian. The building is very old and is positioned on a tiny lane that was used a hundred years ago by nuns going to and from the neighboring small church. In front of the house is a small religious shrine with a crucifix and the German, "Mein Gott, warum hast du mich verlassen?" The shrine has been very well known locally for over a hundred years. So, on our first trip I simply brought a photo of this shrine and asked for directions.

After finding this house for the first time, I was intrigued. As I peered inside of what was now a *trattoria,* a small restaurant, bed and breakfast known as *La Veneta*, I could not help but wonder at how my grandmother managed this large building. After her husband had died and left her with four children, the work load must have been enormous. There are, in fact, two houses that comprise what I knew collectively as *grandma's house in Merano*. The first house is the building that now serves as the small restaurant and *albergo*. It is in decent repair, but its one hundred plus age is starting to show. The second house, directly behind the first, is in shambles and my father told me that this house had always been in poor condition, even in the years immediately after the first world war. My grandmother's brother, Valentino, lived in this second house. He was a lawyer by profession and was fond of advising the family in all legal and financial affairs.

My grandmother had returned from America to Austria (now Italy) with a fair sum of money. Her husband had sold his sheep ranching interests in Wyoming before dying and the family was well off for the times. At the onset of World War I, Valentino the lawyer advised my grandmother to invest all of her money in the war effort. Unfortunately, being Austrian, he talked his sister into depositing the entire family fortune into German War Bonds and of course every schilling was lost. I have often mused at the *what ifs* and wondered how life might have been growing up in a well to do family in Merano. Ah, the fates!

The two houses in Merano form an unbreakable link that binds me to my past. Today, whenever I go to Merano, I gaze at these two old edifices with a great deal of pride. I hope someday to fully understand the tribulations endured by my grandmother in these houses and to more fully understand why I am who I am.

The second house was not as easy to locate. In fact, I could not locate this house during the first three trips to Italy. I searched both the streets of Merano as well as the neighboring suburb of Lagundo to no avail. I asked local officials through long letters from the United States and in person as I stood in their cold stone offices. No trace seemed to remain of what had been loosely described to me as "the villa in Lagundo." I had in fact given up on the idea of finding this old house when I received a pleasant surprise during a lunch at the house of my father's cousin in Merano. As I munched a bit of bite of wonderfully prepared pork cutlets, I asked offhand if she knew anything about this old house. Why, of course she knew everything! Eighty-six year old minds here are a thing of wonder and are, in fact, better than most computers I have used. Without hesitation, Zita told me all about this house, its history and present address. Immediately after lunch, we walked the short distance and stood in front of the *Villa Gustavo*. It is directly on the main street, immediately adjacent to Merano's new Tapainer Hospital. It is technically within the city limits of Merano presently, but was once just within the boundary of Lagundo. Ironically, this property once included all of the land of the present day hospital complex. In its day, the property was a large vineyard.

My father had given me vivid accounts of his earliest memories here in this house. He remembered, remarkably, being bathed as a baby and then placed on a cold marble-topped table to dry. It was really the only thing he remembered of the house, except that his older sister had helped dry him off on this cold table. Apparently, memories are very good in my family for my father could not have been more than months old at the time; his sister died when he was only 8 months old. Although I shared photographs of this house with my father shortly before his death, I was unable to bring him to Italy to see the old house for himself. It was, it seemed, another trace left for me to find but not for others to follow.

I stood in front of this house for a long time, taking pictures from various angles and beaming with pride in my discovery. Then I noticed a rare thing indeed. On the north side of the house, there were words written long ago and covered with many layers of white wash. The letters were peering through in the strong sunlight and gave me another glimpse into my family's past. There on this wall for all of the world to see was a stark condemnation which, when translated, reads: "Italy cares nothing for its people and their well being; she cares only for her pockets." I later learned that indeed this motto of sorts had been placed there shortly after this area, including the house, had been seceded to Italy from Austria at the conclusion of the first world war. Apparently, my grandmother did not like her new government none too much. Her brother, the now disillusioned lawyer, had the words painted boldly for all to see. After losing all of her money on the advice of her brother, my grandmother once again retreated to America where she was already a citizen. Life is often strange and in my grandmother's case, life involved an ever constant yo-yoing from one continent to another. It sounds like fun today, but I am guessing she didn't see it that way over a hundred years ago.

The houses in Merano, La Veneta and the Gustavo, are the traces that were left for me to find and to follow. They have provided me with a great deal of information, history and in the end, a great deal of pride. They were once quite elusive but now they are like old friends, warm and comfortable in my company. These traces, I believe, were left here by my family for me to find; perhaps to point the way, by example, to a new life in a new land. I am thankful.

The Iceman

He sat in the corner booth of the Scoiattolo Albergo in Tret, Italy sipping a glass of red wine with a deliberate sense of ease. His eyes were intense as he argued a small point with his drinking companions and the feather in his Tiroler hat fluttered with each inflection of his voice. Satisfied with his efforts, he reclined into the booth and in an instant smiled briefly at me before returning to his awaiting forum. This was my memorable and brief first glimpse of the iceman.

Later that month, I again arrived at the Scoiattolo for an evening glass of wine of my own and there in the corner he appeared again. This time the smile was bent tersely toward me as if to favor an introduction. But I was new in this part of the world and so I simply smiled back at him without uttering a single word. But his face began to intrigue me for here was an ancient visage in a modern time, his face full of character and his voice strange as my new land. He spoke the local dialect Nones with quick jabs and rarely waited for a retort before forging ahead with a new point. I immediately identified him as a local resident of some social standing but I did not know him at all. He was somewhat short in stature, as is the norm for these parts. He was a man who worked with his hands; this I could tell from the calluses on his fingers and the lines in his forehead. He was a man of the mountains, a glimmer from the past when this part of Italy was the old Tirol and people here were plain spoken and hard working. He was born of the past. Amid his feature rich face was a small mouth, always posed; it seemed, in a sort of a smile. And when he laughed, one could plainly see this man had few teeth between his ruddy cheeks. My first glimpse reminded me of the Iceman, the ancient man of the Tirol who was found frozen in the Italian Alps in 1996. And so I began to refer to this man in that certain sense simply as the Iceman.

I did not see the Iceman for some time after those two initial encounters. He seemed to have disappeared into the forest from which he came. Then, upon my return to Tret a year later, I found him again, still looking the same with the same green felt Tiroler hat. Indeed, I learned that the Iceman was a resident of Tret. He appeared regularly in Tret's small church as part of the choir every Sunday, always with his famous hat in hand. I made small inquiries and learned that he was a member of the volunteer fire department in this small village. But beyond this, I knew nothing, not even his name. I would see him at various gatherings in the community, usually seated by himself in some distant corner of the gathering. He always smiled his small, toothless smile.

When I moved to this small village permanently, again the Iceman was always there in every facet of life in this tiny town. I would see him sipping his red wine into the evening and I would see him in town walking on one of its three streets. But who was this Iceman? He seemed at once foreboding and warm at heart. He would appear as if out of nowhere from his field, *falce* (scythe) over his shoulder like some fragment of a picture of Father Time.

I asked around and through some of my distant relatives I learned that his name was Emilio Bertagnolli. He was in fact of the same surname as many of my cousins, but he was not directly related. Here in this part of the world, many unrelated people share the same surname. It is a common occurrence and not thought of often with any special effort. This man intrigued me and I wanted to know him. However, the opportunity never seemed to come as the Iceman would come and go with the stealth of a night hunter. I would see him briefly and when I sought him out, he was always gone.

After much effort, I did learn that he lived in the lower part of the village and that he owned a *prato* where he would toil into the later summer hours cutting the hay by hand with a *falce*. I once met him on the street as he was walking to his field and he stopped unexpectedly in the middle of the street to greet me enthusiastically. It seemed that although we had not been introduced, he knew much about me. He asked how we were settling into our new home in the mountains above the village and he talked a bit about the recent change in the weather.

All of this tumbled from his mouth in the local dialect, which I could barely understand. The conversation was confounded further by the fact that the Iceman was in good part deaf with only a small ability to hear remaining. I nodded now and then, smiled and tried to move the conversation forward although my attempts proved awkward at best. Finally, the Iceman's hat blew off his head in a sudden gust of wind. I bent down quickly and retrieved it as he simultaneously swung around to grab it narrowly missing my head with his *falce*. Feeling fortunate, I said goodbye and he continued on his way down the street and into his field.

This experience made my mind up more than ever to meet this interesting man and to learn more about him; to get to know this Iceman Emilio. However, time proved again the Iceman to be elusive and it was quite some time before the opportunity once again was right for a friendly introduction.

Oddly, it occurred after Sunday mass one blustery day in October. As I made my way through the front door of the church amongst the crowd, I recognized his red cheeks somewhere close to the rectory door. In an instant, I turned to my right and briskly made my way in deliberate steps to the Iceman. "*Bon Di*," I blurted in the local dialect. He smiled his strange little smile and with a wink of his eye at last we were properly introduced. There was no need for more words. We have been friends ever since.

Postscript: Sadly, my friend Emilio passed away at the age of 82 on September 23, 2007. He is remembered for his humor, wit and above all for his quiet commitment to his community and to his God.

Maestro Marcello

The first time I met Marcello will be burnt in my memory forever. My wife and I were visiting Tret, Italy for the first time in our lives. We had walked through this small village of 278 people, taking pictures and recording a bit on videotape for my father back home in America. As we walked through the streets, narrating the tape, we would hear windows open with a creak and then slam shut as we passed by. It was a bit strange and like walking through a ghost town full of people. After we had finished our first pass though town, we stopped at the *Alimentari* where my father had been born some eighty decades before. As I attempted to communicate in a language of which I had no real command, the door burst open and a little man full of energy strode toward the store owner and asked in Nones, "Where are they.... Where are the Americans?" The woman behind the counter was a bit embarrassed as I was standing behind the door. She pointed awkwardly at me and said, "There!" This man was Marcello and I

45

did not know at the time that our paths would cross many times in the years to come.

We spoke a bit and his curiosity was satisfied. We were, after all, one of the only Americans that had ever visited this tiny part of the world. He rushed out in the same manner in which he had entered and I found his name only by asking the owner of this store. Afterward, my wife and I continued our vacation but the memory of this meeting always remained along with a curiosity to know who this man really was.

Every year for about five or six years, we returned to Tret to pass our free time. Gradually, we began exploring in earnest the idea of moving here for good. It was a big step, but finally we arrived in May of 2003 to set-up residency in northern Italy in the land of my forefathers. There were many things to do initially and many people to meet in this small community. The quickest and best method of meeting people in this situation is to attend the local church regularly, which we did. On our first visit to the Church of Saint Anna, I immediately recognized Marcello from our first meeting. He was always leading the choir in church and seemed very earnest in this endeavor. His hands were busy showing the choir members where to raise and lower their voices. When these untrained voices did his bidding, he was pleased and a small smile escaped his lips. But when a single voice went astray or the organist hit a clinker, an almost unholy frustration passed over this man. At first, I did not know why.

The weeks passed into months and we were ever present at church and so was Marcello. Every Sunday, after mass, Marcello and a group from the choir would gather at the local bar in the Aurora Hotel to go over a few musical notes and share a *buono bianco* or good white wine. My wife and I always followed, but sat apart in a different part of the bar, not wanting to disturb the meeting. After months of the same routine, I finally ventured awkwardly over to their table one Sunday and introduced myself. Introductions are seldom needed here but I felt a need to formally meet this group of people, including Marcello. The stern expression immediately evaporated from his brow and he broke into a broad smile. It seems that he had been just as anxious to meet me and just as unsure about the process. We exchanged stories about the village's past (of which I had become somewhat expert) and talked about the future of the choir and other matters of general interest. As we parted to head to our home for lunch, Marcello made an open invitation to come visit him and his wife at their home.

I saw Marcello again at a town picnic, which is held in a high summer pasture once a year in June. In fact, he was kind enough to offer my wife and I a ride back to town. On the way home, we spoke quite a bit and I finally began to see a glimpse of the full measure of the man. Marcello had been trained professionally as a musician and was a very competent composer of church music. I listened eagerly as he explained that he was part of a regional choir that sang professionally at various church events throughout the valley. As he dropped us off on our street, he again extended an invitation to his home and also asked if we might be interested in an upcoming choir event.

We attended the choir event immediately but it was some time before we were able to visit Marcello at his home. When the time felt right, I timidly knocked on his door several times but without an answer. Bruised knuckles reminded me once again that there are few door bells in this part of the world. A neighbor noticed my dilemma and shouted to Marcello from one second floor building to another to tell him that he had guests. We spent a pleasant afternoon and were fortunate to meet a great many of his many daughters. The afternoon culminated with a tour of his musical studio in which he showed me the sheet music of several of his compositions. To my great surprise and delight, I found that many of the hymns that I had sung in church every week were actually penned by Marcello some years ago. We exchanged a bit about music philosophy, as I too was a writer of music years ago, and sealed the evening with a new friendship.

I was very impressed by Marcello and I continue to admire him. He lives in a modest house, full of hunting trophies including stuffed birds. He is an intense man, always alert and always looking for some new pleasure in life. His musical talents are great and I finally understood why he winced so when the music did not go well in church. He can always hear the music in his head as it was written and should be sung. But, alas life is imperfect and so is the music in our small church.

As Christmas approached, I wondered what small gift I might deliver with our *auguri* (greetings) for the holiday season. I pondered a bit and immediately lit upon an idea. Years before, I had found a poem written by another Bertagnolli from the town of Sanzeno. This poem, Padre Nostro, was written in the native valley dialect of *Nones* a hundred years ago and was one of my favorites. I presented a printed version to Marcello for Christmas long with a suggestion that had long intrigued me. "What do you think about putting this poem to music? I asked. "Aspetta, aspetta," he replied. Then his eyes flashed as he began to see a theme for the score. Yes, I was sure that this was one of the best Christmas gifts that I had ever given.

Elvira

Some things always come in the same color. And like the sky, Elvira always came in blue. Her legs bowed under the weight of her 91 years, she moved about the cobblestones with the ease of a cat. Blink and she was no more, only to reappear further up the street in the shadows of the buildings. Her head was nearly always neatly covered under a scarf, which neatly met her blue sweater. Her bastone (cane) was always at hand but lightly used as this independent soul criss-crossed the tiny streets of Tret.

Every morning would find Elvira seated on the wooden bench near the spot in the piazza (plaza) where the milk was collected from the farmers daily. There in the morning shadows, Elvira held court with the best of her friends, the many cats of Tret. They would assemble in orderly fashion at the first site of the great lady. They knew her well for she always came at the same time bearing a sack of butcher's scraps. There in the morning quiet, the cats would feast and Elvira would once again find happiness. The little ones would soon die anyway she would say with an air of stark reality. She was simply making them happy in the meantime.

I first noticed Elvira in church, where she always occupied the exact same seat. Sundays found her always in blue and always happy. She sang the hymns and took communion each Sunday as the years passed very slowly and steadily here in the mountains. Her hearing was sharp and her eyes were focused like those of her youth. She greeted everyone in town enthusiastically and with vigor. And if you bent closer to share some intimate detail of your week, her eyes would twinkle just a bit before she exploded with laughter, long opinions and good advice. She knew her place well in this tiny village. She was its oldest resident and was sure to have the wisdom that went hand in hand with her years. To share all of this was her duty, perhaps her destiny.

Time passed slowly and late Spring galloped into Summer without notice. The Summer was hot and without rain. It was painfully dry and worrisomely full of daily thunderstorms. Elvira's little cats diminished a few in number but they were ever present in the piazza waiting for their patron. Every morning Elvira would appear, the cats would eat and so the cycle was renewed daily throughout the long season.

But Summer always bends toward Fall with certainty and so when the first snow came to this mountain village, the cats had indeed diminished in number as predicted by their patron. The strong ones had survived but Elvira did not make her appointed rounds in the late Fall and Winter for the weather was simply too bitter for a woman of her years. She disappeared from the church as well, preferring to watch the Sunday services on television. She was devout but not stupid. To risk a fall on the icy cobblestones was not in her best interest and she knew it well.

Having not seen her for some weeks, we became a bit anxious as we missed her wisdom and humor. And so we decided to pay her a visit at her home. As I ascended the old wooden steps to her apartment, warped with the burden of time, I wondered in astonishment how a woman of over 90 years could negotiate these steps daily. The building itself, like the steps, was very old numbering perhaps four hundred years. The stone walls were mortared carefully but clearly showed their age. Bits of crumbling stone and dry rotted wood were everywhere. I knocked on the door and within seconds Elvira appeared and with a great laugh of joy she showed us in. She was, as always, wearing blue.

We spoke a bit and then I presented Elvira with an unusual gift. Days before, I had compiled her family tree into a book of sorts and had inserted a photo of her on the cover. She was clearly pleased as I explained how I had obtained the genealogical information throughout the years to include all of the families of Tret. Like many of the people here, Elvira had not learned much about her ancestry beyond her grandparents but had often wondered about her origins. It turned out that her ancestry and mine crossed paths in two distinct places in the past and that we were in fact distant cousins. This cemented a great relationship and as we left, she presented us with a jar of cherries, which she had canned that Summer. Reciprocal gift giving is an expected norm here and we were very grateful for her thoughts.

I thought of Elvira frequently. She is one of those treasures that you find in life and cherish for the sheer joy it brings. We had become so accustomed to sharing some of our time with her in the Summer, that as the Winter progressed we missed her very much. As Christmas approached, I wondered at what gift might make this woman happy and to know that she was loved by people who only months before had been strangers. I thought of Elvira and looked toward the sky. The two, you see, were always in blue here in Tret. And so we found a nice little blue scarf and it seemed to make the perfect gift. We delivered our Christmas gift without fanfare one afternoon when we spotted Elvira in the piazza. She was moved and through her tears she thanked us profusely. We wanted only for her to know that she was thought of often and fondly by us.

The Winter lingered on for months. The cycle of life here in the Italian Alps is endless and without time. However, in the arctic blue light of the Trentino Winter, all of Tret comes to a halt. Through this pause in time, when the quiet snow gathers on the roof tops, a visage of the woman in blue seems to sneak onto the streets in fleeting glimpses. Yes, there are still many cats that wander the small streets of Tret. Some have gone on to their reward but many have remained in the hope of finding Elvira again.

And yes, that great lady Elvira is still there too. And she is almost always in blue.

Author's Note: In December of 2012, Elvira celebrated her 100th birthday and then passed away just a few days later.

Animali

Our small alpine village is home to many animals (animali) and birds. In this fact we took much delight as I suppose it reminded us of our old home in Eugene, Oregon in the United States where our back yard was always full of deer, raccoons and birds. However, during our first visit to the area in 1997 we did not see a single bird or animal, save a dead squirrel on the road. Strange how time plays tricks on us all!

It wasn't until we started living here that we finally began to see and understand the wildlife that is so abundant in these mountains. We learned there are many animals of the forest that include *cervi* (elk), *caprioli* (deer), *orsi* (bear) and *scoiattolli* (squirrels). Thankfully, there are no raccoons in this part of Italy!

One of our strangest encounters occurred before we were officially residents, on a late night in November, 2002. We were returning from a late night dinner at a friend's house in Senale, a neighboring village further up the valley. We were traveling the *Palade*, the main road connecting our valley to Merano. The road was built in the early 1930's under Mussolini. Coming out of a curve in the road, we spotted something moving in the roadway; it was a cat playing with what looked like a dark colored ball. I stopped the car at the side of the road and investigated. The cat immediately took off into the night, leaving this ball in the middle of the pavement. Then suddenly the ball unrolled itself and walked off into the night. This was my first glimpse of a hedgehog or *riccio* as they are known locally. I had never thought to see one of these strange creatures in Italy as I mistakenly thought they only lived in England. It was a pure joy to see this little animal up close. Luckily, he not been injured by the cat and both sauntered off into a moonless night.

After moving to Tret permanently, one of the first things on our "must do" list was to install a series of bird feeders in our garden, as my wife and I are avid bird watchers.

Once in place, it took only perhaps ten minutes for the birds to start arriving. The Alps are home to a strange mix of birds, some coming from Africa for various parts of the year. The garden was full of interesting species from the beginning and included chickadees (large ones), *gazza ladra* (magpies), red woodpeckers, green woodpeckers and an assortment of smaller birds that defy cataloging. However, our first surprise was the abundance of Cuckoos. These birds, which form the pattern song for the famous clocks, are absolutely everywhere from the month of April through July. They begin their singing in the pre-light hours and continue until the very last light. Sometimes, their endless singing becomes annoying; sometimes their song is like a mountain orchestra that never stops. It is a shame of sorts that they have become so commonplace to us. They are beautiful reminders of the old world Europe and days that have dimmed into history forever.

Half way through of our first year, we visited the nearby German speaking village of Senale on several occasions and witnessed two delightful animal happenings first hand. The first occurred one evening after a short rain. My wife and I had gone to the local meat store to by a few things. Afterward, we paused on the street opposite the store to admire a local resident's garden. Suddenly we heard the quacking of a duck and as we turned around we watched a large mallard make its way over the cobble stoned main street to the front door of a restaurant. The duck sat there in front of the door and quacked up a storm for quite awhile. Finally convinced that there were indeed no handouts to be had, the mallard calmly went quacking back up the street and across the other main road toward the small pond from which it came. Not being one to assign human qualities to animals, I could still not help but wonder if the duck was in fact quaking in German.

The other episode occurred in the exact same location some months later. We were sitting in the restaurant's bar with a friend from Tret around noon. As we finished a glass of wine, I glanced out the door and there in the middle of the street sat a hedgehog. This was no ordinary hedgehog, but a huge specimen with apparently no fear of man nor beast. We bolted out the door for a closer look. Normally this animal will hiss and roll into a protective ball when approached by humans or other animals. Instead, this hearty hedgehog simply continued his rounds, occasionally hunting-up a little food near the roadside. A small crowd gathered around this prickly fellow, drawn by curiosity. Finally our friend removed the hedgehog from the street to prevent it from being accidentally struck by a car. Our small friend made no protest and simply went on its way after it was released in the grass near the road. Finally, it entered a barn that is used by the owner of the meat store. Although I know there is always a large dog in this barn, I heard no noise, no commotion. Perhaps the two were old friends.

We continued to enjoy the abundance of wildlife near our new home. Daily, we learned more new things about our fellow forest dwellers. The changing seasons always brought a new migration of birds from Africa and central Europe. The ever changing bird population was augmented by steady visits from the many mammals that made our garden their home. Winter found elk and deer always on our property looking for food when the snow was deep up on the mountain. The squirrels, once too timid to visit our yard were now regular guests at our bird feeders where they would steal away a great deal of sunflower seeds daily.

People often speak of all creatures, great and small. Indeed, we found them all here in our little piece of the world. They were welcomed for the comfort they brought and in the knowledge that in the end we are all creatures, great and small in the forest of life.

City Folks

Years ago, there was a popular movie in the United States called "City Slickers." It starred Billy Crystal and it was a large hit. The plot centered on a group of young men from a large city who went to a dude ranch to be cowboys for the Summer. In one of its great scenes, Curly (played by Jack Palance) looks at his bewildered charges in the midst of a roundup and exclaims with exasperation, "City Folks!"

I find myself uttering the same words as I curl my lip in the same way that Jack Palance curled his years ago. Ah, but for reasons most different! I live high in the mountains of the Italian Alps, away from the cities. I have always lived away from the cities and the people who live there. As such, I have always preferred as neighbors others who share my respect and love for the outdoors and who know how to balance their lives with the quiet of the mountains. Here, the soft rhythms of nature welcome those who appreciate her beauty but mock those who come merely to play and make noise.

There is nothing inherently wrong with city folks. They are often very nice people. However, they can sometimes collectively belong to a group that expects Disneyland to be found in an alpine meadow and often complains that food tastes better at McDonald's. In short, they are often to be pitied and left to their mouse holes in the big cities below in the crowded valleys.

After moving to Tret we noticed that the toll of parked cars near our house grew each day as we entered Summer. The reason, it seemed, was the small lake above our home. Those from the neighboring cities of Merano and Bolzano often came here for a day trip to the lake as the weather warmed. We live at the end of the road that leads to the hiking trail that in turn leads to this lake. Of this in itself, I have never found complaint. However, as we noticed more and more cars, we also noticed more and more trash thrown about into this sensitive alpine environment. The garbage ranged from candy wrappers to plastic bottles; from cigarette butts to filled trash liners brought from home. As June moved to July then to August, the situation became almost unbearable. Cars numbering from twelve to seventy often blocked the access to our home. I attempted to pick-up the trash that was left about, but the sheer amount proved to be too great. In the end, I was left to only grumble, "City Folks!"

One day in late Summer, I went from my home to my garden to do a bit of work with the vegetables. To my surprise, I found a tourist sitting at our pick nick bench smoking a cigarette and looking bewildered as I approached. I did not know what exactly to say at first. Our garden's perimeter is politely marked with gentle reminders that the property is private. Finally, I asked in Italian, "Can I help you with something?" This man stared back at me as though I was a waiter in a restaurant and muttered "Nein, Ich brauche nicht." City Folks, you see, come in all languages. So I politely asked this man to leave (yes, in German) and suggested the nearby restaurant for his culinary and smoking pleasures.

The home, which we had purchased, was in a building that consisted of four apartments, two on each level of the building. Ours was the *mansarda*, an apartment under the slanted roofline. Throughout our first Summer months, the peace of the Italian Alps was untouched, save the occasional sounds that wafted out into the night from the nearby bed and breakfast. These were golden months of long golden days and they were quiet days. Fall arrived with a change of weather but also with another change. The apartment below us had been sold to a couple from the big city of Trento. Again, City Folks! We hoped for the best but were soon to learn the worst. These people were almost stereotypical in the Italianess. They arrived in a great cloud of dust in their BMW and announced that they were going to settle in Tret to retire. But, of course, there were many changes that they had in mind for our small building; after all, they were from a large city and knew better of such things. I listened, I waited and I smiled.

Then came the sudden bangs at all hours from God knows what and the constant steady hum of a vacuum cleaner from below. Five times a day this great cleaner of the mountains hummed its course below us. Apparently, the poor man had allergies and, of course, moving to the dust of the Dolomite Mountains had not been his greatest decision. I listened, I waited, and I smiled. Fortunately, they only came for the weekends. "City Folks!" I mumbled again and again as the circus continued under my feet.

These poor souls were joined in turn by our other weekend neighbors downstairs and to the left; another couple from a neighboring large city. When the snows came, their parties stopped and they went home early to the cities below us. To come and visit the mountains, like Disneyland, requires no real work. Shoveling snow, on the other hand, does require great effort. As the months progressed, I began to feel as though I would always be haunted by these carrion eaters of the cities.

Time shuffles on and with these short strides patience is usually an unwilling companion. I have come to learn that I really can't change much in this world. The inclusion of City Folks in my otherwise uncluttered life has become a reality; like a faucet that drips just occasionally, it really isn't worth the bother of fixing in the end.

"City Folks!" I have seen my share of this tribe throughout the years, on several continents and in many lands. I don't care to see much of them in the future.

Water, Water, Everywhere
(nor any drop to drink)

The Italian Alps are known for their abundant snow and water. They are the very lifeblood of this green land, from the tallest peaks of the Dolomites to its steps where much of Europe's fruit is grown. Lakes and streams are everywhere and it seems, in the end, that all of this liquid must eventually flow downhill to the greedy mouth of the Po Plain. Like a sponge, the Po and its cities absorb a great deal of this alpine bounty, all without tribute.

We live in a tiny village, positioned at the very top of the Val di Non on the southern flank of these great mountains. We live in the virtual midst of water at an elevation where even the clouds are nearer and ever present. Here one is reminded of the great Rocky Mountains of Montana and Canada. Yet, here the mountains are steeper, their glacier-cut features protruding upward at unbelievable angles. Water cut these fine monuments and water continues to be the vital force in all this land.

After moving here to live, we noticed immediately that public utilities, such as they are, often are found intermittently. During any normal rainstorm, one can regularly depend on the undependability of electricity and lights. Like gnomes in the night, lights here vanish without a trace only to reappear again moments, hours or days later without notice. Then there is the unscheduled maintenance of these public utility gems, usually performed without notice of any kind. These combine to keep a person guessing if they should turn on their computer or not and more importantly, will the wine be chilled for dinner. These mere trifles are dealt with summarily on a day to day basis and no one here really seems to mind that much if there is no electricity or water as long as these come back into the picture at some future date.

Being new to this small village, we initially tried very hard to accept these small inconveniences and take into our stride the differences that make living in the mountains, well, like living in the mountains. Our first experience with electricity came at the expense of a video player that we had purchased new in the United States and then shipped to Italy. We were careful to plug it into a proper current converter and low and behold, it blew-up. At the repair counter at the local electric supply store, I was told matter-of-factly that I needed a much larger converter, and so I paid the repair bill and purchased an unwieldy converter to be used in our bedroom. It was expensive lesson to be sure, but one that I thought worth learning.

A month or so passed by and we were having a birthday party in August for a great-aunt. The weather was unusually unpredictable and a sudden thunderstorm advanced on our tiny abode. With a crack that could be heard around the world, a lightning bolt grounded itself very near our house. I checked for damage and found none. However, when I turned-on my computer two days later, it too began to smoke accompanied by a smirking blink of the cursor now and then. It seemed that the storm had worked its magic on our machine as well. This required a trip to yet another repair shop, located in a not too close town some miles away. We waited anxiously for a week but did not receive the promised phone call with an estimate for repairs. We drove to the shop only to find that the computer had already been repaired, sans estimate, some days ago. The tab for this lesson was even greater as I was told in somber tones, "Everyone here knows that you have to unplug all of your electronic items every time a thunder storm grows near!" Well, I didn't know before the incident, but I sure do know now.

Electronic digital clocks are one of our modern miracles. But I tell you honestly, they are no great wonder when the electricity goes off every six or so days and the clocks must all be reset. This tedious work was performed numerous times within the first three months of our arrival. Tick-tock, tick-tock! Time is money here as everywhere and we certainly spent quite a lot resetting our four digital clocks.

We return now to water. As I stated, it is everywhere. Everywhere, except perhaps where it should be the most: in my tap ready to flow into my waiting glass. You see, repairs here to the domestic water system are made rather regularly but without an ounce of notice. The great fluid of life simply ceases for undisclosed amounts of time only to reappear at whim of a local bureaucrat at some later date. When the water quits, it has a pinball effect on other things in your life. A shower, for instance, becomes the impossible dream. The hot water heating system is hot but without water. In short, the whole carousel stops in mid circle and begs that we all get off.

After several of these water episodes, I began to ask questions of my neighbors. Was this normal? Didn't it hurt business? Did anybody care? Yes, no and no. I was finally left to accept the situation for what it was; a new aspect of living that had to be learned if not liked. However, as I looked around me at all of the abundant water in the sky, the lakes and the streams, I could not help to wonder if Coleridge was right and

that perhaps I was wrong. Perhaps I needed
a bit more convincing.

Linguistics at Lana

The gentle sounds of Peter, Paul and Mary's "Blowin' In The Wind" filtered out the door and onto the cold cobblestone streets of Lana. Lana is a small community near Merano, Italy, set in the foothills of Italian Alps. We had traveled here on our way back to our home from nearby Bolzano to sample some unexpected cuisine. Three weeks earlier, we had stopped at the same location only to find that Monday was indeed the *Ruhetag* (day off). Undeterred, we returned. The sign above the door said "Asia Point Bangkok – Bar and Restaurant." Looking harmless enough, we stepped through the door to give it a try.

We immediately knew that this was not what we had expected. This restaurant was no mere knock-off of Asian cuisine…. It was the real deal! The menu was full and richly textured with a variety of Asian dished from Thailand, China and Japan. We were seated at an interesting table made of ironwood, complete with carved matching chairs. The waitress who seated us spoke excellent High German and so I returned the favor of her language with all of the ability and grace that I could muster. However, I must admit that it seemed a bit unusual to be speaking German in a Chinese restaurant in Italy. Eagerly, we scanned the menu and ordered a couple of dishes that I thought especially unusual in this part of the world. Again, the German interplay seemed strange as I ordered the Tom Yom Kum soup from Thailand and the sushi from Japan. Yet, everything was in its place. The German language did not adversely affect the Japanese pronunciations of the various sushi and so we moved forward into the meal with vigor.

While we waited for our first course to arrive, I fiddled with the chopsticks that were left at our table along with the silverware. Over the years, I have become expert at using these delightful little tools. As I opened the package in which they were enclosed, I noticed another strange thing. The directions for using the chopsticks were printed unmistakably in French, a language which I speak poorly. The directions were printed on the outside of the package and included various diagrams on how to use *Les Baguettes*. Intrigued, I couldn't help but wonder at the immense variety of language that we were experiencing in the course of an evening out. I was beginning to feel quite cosmopolitan as I whizzed through dinner amidst the majority of the European languages. It was beginning to be a truly *buona serata* (good evening), *mit gut essen* (with good food) and full of a lot of colorful sounds.

As we ate our way through the evening, the music continued in waves of the English language, of which we had heard very little for months. Then a second waitress approached our table as the first woman was now busy with a large party of other guests. She addressed me in Italian. This is not unusual here, as we were in the dual language province of Bolzano. However, this young woman spoke only Italian and so I switched gears a little and continued on in Italian, securing at last the rest of our meal. The food arrived accompanied by of waves of German, Italian, Thailandian, Chinese and Japanese. I was becoming a bit dizzy with the experience but was determined to press on.

Between courses, I kept staring at a photograph that hung on the wall above me. It had apparently been taken many years ago and features two women, one of whom was Thailandian. The other's face was strangely familiar but I simply could not place it. Besides, we were in Italy and I was sure that the familiarity of the face was simply coincidental. Again and again I glanced up at the photograph. Very familiar! I finally stood up and peered at the photo closely. "My God," I exclaimed to my wife. "That's Liz Taylor!" We both looked at the photo over and over, trying to figure out why such a photo was on the wall.

Finally, the owner of the restaurant came over to our table to speak to us. We complimented him on the quality and authenticity of the food. He was speaking English, with an Austrian German accent. I inquired as to where he was born and it turned-out that he was born in Innsbruck, Austria. The language element of our evening was ever broadening and I was pleased. I asked if the photo was indeed of Elizabeth Taylor. He looked up at the photograph beamed. "You are the first people who have ever recognized Elizabeth Taylor in this photograph," he flatly stated. Then he went on to explain the origin of the photo. It seems that years ago, his grandmother had helped Miss Taylor in her home while filming a movie on a foreign location. The picture was simply a souvenir and gesture of thanks offered by Miss Taylor. We spoke for some time to the restaurant's owner on a wide variety of subjects. He explained further that his two waitresses each spoke only one language but that together they covered the range of languages spoken locally and that was all that mattered in the end. I agreed.

Satisfied and full, we moved slowly from our table to the lobby to pay our bill. I thanked the owner in English, the waitress in German, the other waitress in Italian and we made our way to the curb. Once again, the chorus from "Blow'n in the Wind" rumbled forth from the interior of the restaurant as we headed for our car. I glanced back a moment for a final look at the restaurant and then I turned my eyes slowly to the high mountains and dark sky that sat above the valley. Somewhere in the shadows was our home. I searched my tired head for a fitting description of the evening. "A*usgezeichnet*" (excellently done!) was the only word that finally came to mind.

Revò

Revò is a medium sized village that lies on what is known as the Terza Sponda (third bank) of the Val di Non. It has been famous for all sorts of things throughout history, from being the focal point of the Rustic Wars of 1525 to being the home to many important people in the world of arts and sciences. However, above all it is one of *our* villages and home to several good friends. Revò has the accent on the last syllable and is pronounced "Ray-Voh." This is handy to know as there are several villages here that accent the last syllable in the same manner.

We had passed through Revò several times during our first visits to the Val di Non, chiefly because it was on the way from the valley's largest city, Cles to Cloz. Because Cloz is my ancestral home, we found ourselves on this part of the pavement many times during all of our trips here. During one of these trips in 1999, my wife wanted to use the bathroom as we passed through Revò. I stopped the car in the local *Piazza* (plaza) and inquired of the owner of a bar there if my wife could use the toilet. She agreed and my wife went off to the bathroom, only to reappear several short minutes later with a strange look on her face. "You won't believe this!" she exclaimed. "You've got to go see the bathroom for yourself." I excused myself and headed off for the john. I opened the door only to gaze with astonishment at the toilet; it was, in fact, a porcelain hole in the floor. More precisely, it was a toilet of a bygone era, made of porcelain in the form of a bowl and placed level with the tiled floor as to require a contortionist for its use. It had little raised ridges on each side, I assumed, to keep one's ass from sliding completely off the pot and sprawled legged onto the floor. Because neither my wife nor I had ever seen such a device, we referred to it simply as "the hole at Revò."

When we returned to the United States that same year, we told this odd tale of the "hole at Revo'" to our friends and family. My mother-in-law, a dear woman with a sublime sense of humor, suggested that we take a picture of this little monument during our next trip. And so we did. During our next excursion to the town, I politely asked if I could use the bathroom in the bar. Once inside, I pulled my camera out of my pocket and took two photographs, forgetting that the flash could be seen in the bar by the owner and all of its patrons. As I left the bathroom, all eyes were upon me. I was embarrassed for these nice people suspected that this crazy American had been admiring himself closely in their bathroom and had taken photos as proof of the act. What could I say? I hurried out into the square wary of a lynch mob that never followed. I brought the souvenirs back to the United States where they adorned a photo album in my mother-in-law's home for many years.

After this initial experience with Revò and its hole, we gradually became interested in learning more about the community in earnest. We had noticed, for instance, that the town had undergone a large rebuilding of its main street with many new additions and conservations of older buildings. We also took note of the town's history. At the town's *municipio* (city hall), the famous

Tirolean Andreas Hofer made a plea for the unification of troops from the Val di Non and Val di Sole in 1808. Today, Revò is home to one of the Val di Non's only remaining vineyards, specializing in wine from the ancient Gropèl grape. In short, we came to know Revò as a progressive community with a blend of a rich past and vibrant future.

Revò is also known as the one village in all of the Val di Non that was host to the largest number of its inhabitants leaving for the Americas in the latter part of the nineteenth century. As much as thirty percent of this village left for the United States, Brazil, Argentina and Canada, to name only a few of the destinations. The ship registers of Ellis Island in New York are filled with the names of families from Revò: Magagna, Martini, Facinelli, Ravina, Rizzi, Flor, Flaim, Iori and countless others. Revò also differs from many of its neighboring villages in that many of these families returned years later to their homes in Revò. It is now home to a fair number of English speaking people who were either born abroad or lived abroad in English speaking countries.

We began to know Revò in its fullest after we settled permanently to the Val di Non. My wife became a member of an English speaking women's group, whose majority were residents of Revò and its sister village of Romallo. We made weekly trips to this village and gradually learned much about its history and culture. All villages in the Val di Non have a *sopranome* or nickname. The *sopranome* for those who live in Revò is *ballarini* or dancers, owing to Revò's past history of the music and dance. It is in fact today home to the Banda Terza Sponda, one of the largest and most prestigious musical bands in all of Northern Italy.

One of these women, in particular, became a good friend. She is Tiziana Ravina and she is a native of Revò who was raised in Halifax, Canada. She later returned to her native village and married a local doctor, Paolo Ziller. She is a delightful blend of Canadian and Nones who can handle herself equally well in either language as well as

French. She is a teacher by education and a bakery chef by passion. Her cookies and *dolce* (sweets) are the enviable products of her mother's love and she is fortunate to have her mother living close by to serve as parent, friend and teacher. Like many people of the Val di Non, Tiziana requires a bit of knowing in order to understand her. Once she reveals herself to you, the Canadian "eh" is understood as the wink of the Nones, the universal sign of accord. She is smart, witty and delightfully Nones.

Revò is the counterpoint to our tiny village of Tret. Revò sits in the lower valley near lake Giustina at an elevation one half of Tret's. When it snows in Tret, it usually rains in Revò. When the fog covers Revò, the sun bathes Tret. Tret is tiny and Revò is large. However, like counterpoint, the two form a harmony with one another and are integrally connected. The *sopranome* (nick name) *Tretter* is found in a few of Revò's households while in Tret, one of the largest and oldest families was once from Revò's nearby village of Tregiovo.

Since we came to live here in the Val di Non, we have come to know many things. Tirolean is not Italian; the *Noce* is a river named for a nut; home is where one eats his *lucanica* (local sausage) and drinks his *teroldego* (local wine); and holes or no, Revò is one of "our villages" and we are proud of her and her people. Truisms are hard-won here and we have been fortunate to learn these in good time. Revò is the centerpiece of our lower valley and has provided us with many of life's small joys.

Mangia! Mangia!

To eat in Italy is to experience one of its true joys. It is always accompanied by a forceful chorus of Mangia! Mangia! (eat! eat!). This is the Italian way of encouraging their guests to eat with the same vigor as local residents. Being new to this part of the world, we were a little hesitant at first but soon learned by force of nature to eat as though we were born in Italy.

One of our first dining experiences in Italy, outside of a restaurant, was at the home of my *pro-Zia* (great-aunt) Zita. In fact, Zita is not my great-aunt but rather the first cousin of my father. She lives in a darling apartment in the center of Merano's city center and it was there that we arrived during our second trip to Italy to dine, as it was destined, with the Gods. Zita had helped cook in the family business years ago and like most women her age in this part of the world, she had learned how to cook most excellently. We had arrived for lunch, or *pranzo*, and in this part of the world, this is the big meal not to be outdone by the mere triflings of dinner or *cena*. She first presented us with intriguing appetizers and wine, which in themselves could have been the meal. I hesitated a bit, not wanting to be too eager. "Managa, Mangia!" came the command from the kitchen. I obediently complied.

Next came the soup, a delicious blend of garden vegetables pureed with just the right hint of spices. Again, "Mangia, Mangia! It will get cold if you don't eat!" Again, I rushed to my plate. By now, however, I was beginning to get a little full; after all, I was still an American with American eating habits. I had already consumed more than an average lunch for the States. The plates and bowls kept coming from behind the kitchen door and I kept eating. After a marvelous array of pasta (primo piato) and meat dishes (secondo piato), a salad arrived in front of me. A bit strange, I thought at first, as the salad is usually the opener in America. Here in Italy, it is actually used to clean the pallet and aid digestion. I paused, then I ate again.

By now, I was sure that I would soon explode when Zita strode through the door carrying desert and spoons. "Mangia, Mangia!" As I finally finished this simple lunch, I felt finally worthy, as though perhaps I had completed the New York Marathon in record time.

As my experience here broadened a bit, I gradually became more accustomed to large lunches and later dinners. Lunch here is always at precisely noon; to do otherwise is considered a *peccato* (a sin) and is avoided at almost all costs. It is sometimes amusing to watch a group of men here in public as the noon hour bell strikes in the village square. They anxiously look at their watches and, with the bewilderment of blind mice, dash off to their homes, perhaps in fear that their wives are waiting with wooden spoons in hand. Again, to be late for lunch is simply not accepted here. Dinner is another thing all together. It usually occurs later than in the United States. The hour varies a bit from host to host and to the time of the year but generally commences between 7 p.m. and 9 p.m. I once had dinner here at a person's house that started at about 9:30. To be honest, as the first course passed into my gullet, I was ready for bed. To me, this time of night is for sleeping not for eating. Yet, I could hear it coming before it arrived: "Mangia, Mangia!"

Lunch or dinner here is almost always followed by *grappa*. This strong liquor is distilled from the mash left over from the wine making process; it is, in fact, distilled grape mash. It comes in many flavors from the pure grape *grappa*, to the prune *grappa* for which Tret is known from far away, to the many flavored versions of this brew that suit the more civilized pallet. I almost always choose something new or at least home made. *Grappa* here is designated to be the finishing touch to a great meal and as such it is to be savored a bit in the process. I always politely take my time; however, it is equally appropriate here to belt the whole glass down in one lifting.

I have had great grappa and not so great grappa here. I have had the homemade prune product that is famous in Tret and I have had the mirtillo (blueberry) brew that goes down so smoothly. In fact, I have probably had, at one time or another, almost every grappa known under the Tirolean sun. Once, I even had a glass or two of grappa that reminded me too much of siphoning gas. However, it was homemade and the host was most proud of his creation and so I drank it with enthusiasm. Where ever I have had *grappa*, I have enjoyed it. However, when the glass is lifted, the chorus here changes slightly to, "Dai, Dai!" (go, go!) and it compliments and counterbalances "Mangia, Mangia!"

Among Tret's many older residents, most men brew some of their own *grappa* every year. It is a rite of passage here high in the mountains and a custom that is timeless. There are serious makers of the brew and weekend distillers who aim only to please themselves with a few bottles. If you are fortunate enough to draw a dinner invitation here, you will almost assuredly be presented with a glass of this mountain madness. Study the face of the host closely. He will almost always wait for your response after the first sip. Proper comebacks include,

"Fortissima!" (strong!), "Buona!" (good!) and "Ottima!" (great). Pay the compliment for it is always deserved.

The eating and drinking experience changes a bit when you visit a restaurant here. The food is prepared and delivered to your table in the same constant, caring manner. However, you are usually left alone to recite the "Mangia, Mangia!" chorus with your dining partners. And because the food was prepared in an anonymous kitchen, it is also considered polite if you simply say nothing and eat. However, if the food starts to cool, I am sure you will hear that chorus in your head anyway.

The enthusiasm for eating and drinking is alike in any household here at any meal at any time of the day. It is largely based on the old Tirolean practice of "living large" (when times allowed). People here, whether rich or poor, will always put a meal in front of you that is fit for kings. To eat here in Italy's Alps is an adventure that changes daily with new delights. Italy is life and the

Tirol is its heart and both are sustained by the plate. Enjoy! But remember, "Mangia, Mangia!"

Postscript: My dear Zita passed away at the age of 98 on August 10, 16 four days short of her 99th birthday. She was a true joy and inspiration to our lives in a new country. The memory of her girlish giggle, uncommon culinary talents and love will remain with us forever.

Pace and Alka-Seltzer

I stood in Tret's small four hundred-year-old church for the first time and trembled a bit at the thought that my father had been christened here nearly ninety years ago. As churches in our valley go, Tret's is not the biggest, neither the prettiest nor the best endowed with wealth. It is, however, a monument to the people of this small community and a testament to their perseverance. The cracking walls are painted with pictures from the bible over a white wash that is curling in places. The pews are care worn from the faithful and the painting of Saint Anna that hangs over the altar is badly in need of cleaning and restoration. However, this is our church and the very nerve center of this village.

Any Sunday begins about the same here. There is a mad dash for the ten o'clock mass. I am always early or at least on time. Others straggle in until well after the first hymn and the pews are always packed to capacity. I sit in the back to the left, a space reserved for the new and infirm of this community. Social rank seems to dictate the seating chart and the community's best known are always in the front rows where God can bestow his blessings to the fullest. Someday, I hope to change my seat.

The little church choir is composed of one true musician and several somewhat reluctant volunteers who sing the hymns off key but with true intentions. The new organ player here is a teenager of perhaps 15. He would rather be playing rock and roll in some distant concert hall I am sure, but he does his part willingly if not accurately in the musical sense. He is one of God's children and as such he is forgiven for his musical shortcomings. I do feel a sense of compassion for the choir leader. He is Marcello, a man in his early eighties who has had a vast musical education and now must endure the purgatory of trying to teach the untalented how to sing. The job is always done well in the end and the end is all that matters much here high in these mountains.

The *parroco* or parish priest is devout and steadfast as he reads from the scriptures. He is also a man of reality and sprinkles his sermon with generous does of local news. He is the people's priest. However, I find later that Don Franco is only here for the Summer and that he returns to his native Bologna every September. He is a very likable man and he makes going to church a pleasure. He will be missed.

Somewhere in the proceeding, about 7/8 of the way through as I reckon, the priest stops and solemnly asks that the congregation exchange greeting of peace, or *pace*. This directive being given, each of the parish extends his or her hand to the people nearest and exclaims "pace." At this juncture, it is an almost certainty that someone will cough in his hand before extending it to his neighbor. After all this is a small mountain village and people often come to church sick. The heat is rarely turned on and the church's cold stone walls only add to the chill, even in the Summer months.

Of this *pace*, there is usually born a cold or two and I have certainly received my share. Sunday is followed by Alka-Seltzer and this poor brew is followed by another Sunday and so the cycle here continues. For months I was either sick or recovering from one cold after another. Usually, when I was feeling a little better someone coughed, extended me his *pace* and I became sick all over again. This continued for so long that I eventually referred to going to church as "*going for a dose of pace.*"

One particular man always sat behind me and for our first initial months in Tret, he always seemed to have a cold. Week after week, we exchanged *pace* and I was usually left a little less healthy for the experience. I did not know this man's name and simply referred to him as the *Pace Man* from Tret. As time moved on, I spoke more and more to this man. He was one of Tret's younger people, perhaps in his thirties. I guessed him to be of the Bertagnolli family, but I never found the proper moment to ask his name. Names here are assumed and rarely spoken of directly. Everyone knows everyone else, but formal introductions are elusive at best. And so I wondered.

After six months or so, I was finally determined to know this individual, as I should, by his rightful name. I went to Sunday mass on the third Sunday of the Advent and there he was, sitting directly beside me for the first time. I could not let the opportunity escape me so I bolted from the pew immediately after the last hymn and stopped him just outside the church door. "Hello," I said, "My name is Allen Rizzi." "I know," he replied casually. I ventured a little further. "You know, we have been neighbors for over a half a year and I don't know your name." His reply was instantaneous; "My name is Claudio." I queried a bit further, "*Cognome?*" "Bertagnolli," he replied simply with a shrug of his shoulders. And so I came to know another of my neighbors in this small village, one Claudio Bertagnolli, a.k.a. *Pace Man*.

As for the Alka-Seltzer, I have found that I am in constant need of this elixir as this is a village full of *Pace*. To attend church here is to love God and your neighbor and embrace a bit of fizzy water with good grace. Perhaps in the future I will suggest to the *parroco* that a vitamin C wafer be substituted for the traditional communion wafer and that Theraflu be substituted for the wine. But for now, for me every Sunday brings a bit of *pace* and *Alka-Seltzer*.

Dying and Paved Streets

The day was dark but it had not rained. It was one of those odd days that set itself between Summer and Fall, failing in the end to be of either. It was lackluster in its entirety except for the fact that a special funeral was to take place in the village. It was our first funeral since moving to our new home, so we were somewhat apprehensive as to how to conduct ourselves. We eventually chose to dress down a bit with the realization that this was a local affair in a very small locality, exempt from some of the city formalities that we were used to. After dressing with some procrastination, we made our way down the hill and into the village proper.

The streets were clogged with cars and great masses of people. They had come from many miles away, from villages and towns near and far, to say goodbye to the *Fandovere*, Vittorio Iori. The population of this tiny village had been doubled within an hour to almost four hundred people. They came from Vittorio's hometown of Tregiovo far down in the valley, from the neighboring large village of Fondo and from wherever this man had family and friends. The funeral itself was a traditional funeral mass that culminated with each attendee sprinkling a bit of blessed water upon the coffin as it lay in the midst of Tret's tiny cemetery. The deceased's sister, the surviving matriarch of the family, greeted each guest with true appreciation for their thoughts and prayers as she made her way sadly from the cemetery to her home. And then it was done.

Fandovere was the *sopranome* or nickname that the Iori family had inherited a century ago after moving from Tregiovo to Tret. The exact meaning of the name had been obscured by time. They were a well respected, large family of many hands who had eagerly worked the earth here for decades in the toil of farming. Their farm was perhaps the largest in the entire village and a source of much pride. Vittorio had not been well for some years, suffering from chronic asthma and a host of other problems. Ironically, we had been guests at his house only days before and we were shocked at his passing. He seemed to have been in good spirits and fair health only days before his death. Life here is often deceptive.

Odd was the day and odd too were the circumstances of the burial. Here in the alpine mountains, land is a precious commodity. And so, when a person dies and is buried another person must make room for the new arrival. Inarticulately put, one person's grave is dug up to make room for the new body. This was a new experience for us and so, in passing the pile of freshly dug earth, we could not help but gasp a bit as we saw bits of old bone and clothing appear from beneath the dirt. This was, after all, someone's father or mother. At first it seemed totally bizarre. But after a lengthy explanation, we were satisfied that we were not about to change centuries of tradition and history. Still, it seemed strange at least and one older aunt concurred that it appeared a bit disrespectful of the dead to have them strewn about the cemetery on the day of another's funeral. At last the day ended with a grateful sigh of relief and all was settled as it had always been.

Two weeks later, the Tirolean Summer had finally died too and the threat of the first snow hid in the cold mountain peaks that surround this valley, the Val di Non. Returning from Fondo on Tret's small main road, we were stopped by the now familiar man with the red paddle. He stood in the middle of the street to block traffic so that the paving crew could finish the job of putting down fresh asphalt on what had been a dirt side road. As we waited in the car, we noticed that this fresh black lane led directly to the house of the *Fandovere*. Such public works usually take a very long time here to actually be completed. Strange, I mused. One must actually die here before his street is paved. In a world where one can set a clock by the imprecision on which everything is run, it was comforting to note that streets did get paved in the end. However, my wife had the last word as usual. "You know, our street was newly paved almost a month ago!"

Nones Smones

Every now and then, I must confront the topic of language. Well, actually more than every now and then, for I live here at the linguistic crossroads in the Italian Alps where my native English is a mere rumor and where I must constantly combat consonants and vowels for my very survival. In this daily struggle, I must race between English, Italian, German and at least two dialects with the grace and charm of an unfettered gazelle. It is a fact of life known as *living here*.

In this small village in this small valley, I am also the resident English teacher and ipso-facto expert of all things American and of the English language. It is a position of privilege and burden that soon exhausts the mind at every turn. It has become my job to not only to explain the American language but to explain the American political landscape as well. I have, therefore, stood solemnly on street corners expounding on American colloquial speech and moments later had to flatly state that it was not George Bush's desk under which lurked the infamous Monica Lewinsky. It seems Americans, as well as their language, are muddled mysteries here.

My English is American English and that makes it almost a totally unknown element hereabouts. What little English local residents have heard has usually come in the form of the very occasional British tourist. Compounding this fact is that what little of my native language is taught here in the secondary schools is exclusively offered in the *British Isles* version. I have therefore, on many occasions, waxed poetic about the virtues of both brands of my language; pointing out with natural pride that American English is superior to that other language they speak in England. I have also explained that a *rubber* in Briton is an entirely different thing in the United States. (I suppose in the end, both have the same effect of cancellation!) I have often delighted in such discrepancies between our two tongues and have had genuine fun explaining the differences when I could find an English speaker who would listen.

In my role as English linguist par excellence, I am also called upon to guide visiting American tourists, translate for them and generally show them a good time. I do this with joy, for it is not often that I get the privilege to hear my native idiom here high in the Alps. However, this also employs working skillfully with the native languages here and that is where the real fun begins. For language here is a sort of private thing, needed at home but shunned a bit in public. Dealing with the multiple languages here is a bit like dealing with the United Nations. There are national and local prides at stake but there must exist some form of common communication. Therefore, these days start early and are exceedingly long. Throw in a couple of lost German hikers from Hamburg and at the end of the day, you might hear me mumble in confused tones something like, "*Um Gottes willen*, this day is finally *finito…. speriamo*!" (God willing, this day is finally done… we hope!).

However, I did not move here to convert my fellow Tiroleans or European tourists to be English speakers. Quite to the contrary, I came here to live amongst them and speak their varied and colorful languages. I have listened intently and I have constantly ventured far out on the fragile language limb to absorb these new sounds. Since most people here speak at least two languages with ease, I am a bit envious and I would like to prove myself equally worthy in the world of words. And so I have struggled to learn what may well be un-learnable. After years of honest effort, I have achieved proficiency but not parity. I must confess that the task may just be a wee bit too big for this American.

The language here is mixed currently between Italian, German and Ladin with literally hundreds of dialects that to the non-native speaker just as well might be Greek. When I moved to this tiny speck on the planet some years ago, I thought I was linguistically well prepared. I spoke German fluently, having studied it intensely in college and I had managed to learn passable

Italian. However, the first time I ordered a couple of beers in the neighboring German-speaking village of St. Felix, I found that *zwei mal bier* (two beers) wasn't connecting. I inquired. It seems that *zwei* is *zwoa* and *mal* is *mul* here and that I might well have saved that college credit money years ago. But I am persistent and I gradually learned some of this German dialect in an effort to fit in, be recognized but mainly to amuse myself. With some measure of success, I do not cringe now when I hear someone call out, *"Wie gets?"* (how's it going?) instead of "Wie ghet's?"

The German dialect that is spoken here is slightly similar to that spoken in Vienna. It is a simple low German, made of many non-German sounding words that baffles even the tourist direct from Munich. It is an old, old German of the mountainous Tirol. To the uninitiated, it sounds brutal and confusing. Conversation here in a bar for instance often contains a certain amount of play on words that only a local speaker will understand. It does have its charm. Responses often begin with a long, drawn-out *e-yoh* as opposed to the standard clipped German *ja, ja* and thus form more romantic rhythms of speech. It also seems to command respect. I have often imagined Andreas Hofer, our Tirolean hero uttering this dialect in his final words as he was lead off to be shot in Mantua. One could argue all day long about the differences between this dialect and its distant cousin, *Hochdeustch* (high German). But in the end, one can only say, *"Aber, was kann Man mach?"* (What can one do?)

Then there is our *local* dialect, that is to say the Italian dialect spoken here in my village of Tret. It is known collectively as Nones in all of its dozens of dialect manifestations. Each village has its own special dialect, its own special form of tormenting me when I try to communicate. It is an ancient language, made partly from Ladin, Latin, Italian and German and God only knows what else with hard, clipped pronunciations. A lot of it, frankly, seems to bare little connection to any of its forefathers. Cheese, *formaggio* in Italian is *formai* in Nones. Give me the key, *Dami l'chiave* in Italian becomes *Dami clau. Guarda!* (look!) is *varda, chiama* (called) is *clama* and after a day or so of this, I am always eager to go to bed early and dream of something simpler and safer like sky diving without a parachute.

Nones is an ancient language and so are many of its speakers. It is a language onto itself that tends to be without tense, straightforward and harsh to the ear. It is spoken with a twinkle in the eye and a bit of *contandino* (farmer) highbrow. Here it is also frequently punctuated with *Madonna* (the Virgin Mary), said with surprise for emphasis. And then there are the myriad variations of *Porco* (filthy pig)*: Porco Madonna, Porco Zio* (uncle)*, Porco Cane* (dog)*, Porco Puttana* (whore)*, etc.* I have tried to devise my own system of learning this brutal piece of work but to little avail. Rules don't exist and alas, there is no textbook. To complicate my efforts as an eager learner, each village has a different version of this inferno so as I go down the valley from one place to another, my feeble attempts at linguistic parity always seem to fail. I found that in Cloz, the village of my ancestors, the residents speak two distinctly different dialects, as one originated in each of its two parishes. I may be quoting Einstein here: "Who knew?"

I soon learned that Nones is also spoken as sort of a secret language. That is to say, that if a local resident wants not to be understood by an outsider, he puts on his secret Nones decoder ring and whirls away with his brethren in the relative security that he will not be understood by tourists and *stranieri* (foreigners) alike. Ah, but I've caught-on quite a bit and can now glean most of the salient bits from any Nones conversation. But this evokes a bit of fear and suspicion at best. I mumble something in my newfound dialect and give them a knowing nod, as if to say, "*capices*!" (understood). But nobody has awarded me a linguistic triple cross yet.

To the credit of my friends and relatives here, they all seem eager to speak standard Italian with me. It is sometimes as hard for them to master this act as it is for us, but in the end we all try hard to communicate and usually succeed. Indeed, a person who has spoken Nones their whole life finds it hard to shift into standard Italian and I sincerely appreciate the effort. As with any two different languages, there are certain words that just don't easily translate from one to another. These occasions produce the *lingua mista* (mixed language) that I have come to hear and appreciate so much. A conversation might begin in standard Italian and then move hurriedly into Nones, proceeding to hand gestures punctuated with *"Sai, Sai?"* (You know? You know?) Or it might begin in German and end in Italian. Or it might even have a word of two of English thrown in as a desperate attempt at spicing-up the dialog. I have been a witness and willing participant in each of these situations. It is confusing, exhilarating and fatiguing. At the end of the day, I always go to bed weary but a bit wiser for my efforts.

Language was initially developed for simple communication. So in the end, I say Nones Smones, lets pick a language or a variant of several and get down to the business of talking, understanding and enjoying life over a bottle of good wine. The rest, in the end, is mere words.

Pluses and Minuses

Living anywhere in this world has its pluses and minuses. We found this to be equally true in the Italian Alps as anywhere else we had ever lived. Each day brought new joys and new frustrations. Another would bring new surprises, both good and bad. Throughout our first year living in the small village of Tret, we compiled the top-ten list of what was good and what was not so good. Here is what we came up with (in no particular order):

Pluses (The Good)

1. The people – This is the truest asset of this land. The people here are marvelous, friendly and lovable.

2. The food – Much has been said of Italian food. True Tirolean food is much better and must be tasted rather than described. Try the *Canederli* (dumplings).

3. The scenery – Each mountain here is literally prettier than the last…. And

there are a lot of mountains. The scenery makes you glad to be alive.

4. The roads – Italy is known for its wonderfully maintained roads. They are a joy to drive on.

5. The History – This area is one of the historically richest of all in the world and you don't have to be a college professor to enjoy it.

6. Restaurants – They are different here and better than those in America. You are purchasing the table for the evening if you wish and no one will give you the *bum's rush*.

7. Language – Here it is always a mix and it is fun to *dig-in* to a bit of the many cultures through the many languages they represent.

8. The Quiet – There is more of this to be found here than most places you can visit. Find your moment and enjoy it!

9. The Wildlife – The amount of animals, plants and flowers here is truly remarkable and a testament to the willingness of these people to preserve them.

10. Family – This is the basis of all life here and it is shared readily with locals and tourists alike. It is the very hallmark of the Tirol.

Minuses (The Bad)

1. The *Intervallo* – This three hour lunch break from twelve to three is a grand waste of time and the largest excuse here for not getting things done.

2. The Driving – One must have a bit of a death wish to drive in Italy. Driving too fast is the norm and watch out for those other guys coming at you in your lane. And stop signs? Forget about it!

3. Lunedì – Mondays here bring another surprise… all the businesses are closed! (Also beware of Thursday afternoons and unannounced closures!)

4. Introductions – There aren't any. You are supposed to know everyone by sight and names are not important.

5. *Stronzo Paper* – These are the toilet paper scraps that one always sees by the side of the road because (alas) there are no public restrooms here.

6. Car Insurance – (or the lack thereof) Very expensive and it covers practically nothing unless you cause the accident. (Remember, three times …. Mia colpa, mia colpa, mia colpa!)

7. Large Cities – By in large, they are dirty, humorless and without a place to park your car.

8. Real Estate – Despite what has been written in other books, there are no deals here! It is expensive, confusing and best

left to escapees from the insane asylum with good accountants and deep pockets.

9. The Euro – One must constantly remember that prices basically doubled when the Euro replaced the Lira. Oh yes, then add that pesky exchange rate of between 20 and 50 percent!

10. Television – If you are a TV junky, beware! The programs don't really start at the time printed in the newspaper. This is just a little inside joke, probably perpetrated by media magnet and Presidente del Consiglio, Silvio Berlosconi.

To sum up our experience here, one could begin by borrowing from Dickens: "these were the best of times, these were the worst of times." In between the extremes of heartache and ecstasy, we have found a life that few have dared to dream and fewer still have achieved. It has come with much work and very high costs but then all things in life are such. We have enjoyed our world here with all of its wonderful aspects and imperfections. Each day has been a true adventure and we are fortunate to have been able to live this dream.

We have been asked many times, over the years, why move to a tiny village in the Italian Alps? These questions have come from people and friends on both continents. The short answer has always been, "*Questa e' la nostra terra*! (This is our land!) Our land in mind and spirit and where we have willed it to be our home. It is not for everybody; it has been, however, for us.

All in all, it has been *quasi perfetto* (almost perfect).

The First Year Ends

Everything has a beginning and an end. Our new life in Italy began with our arrival in Tret on May 21, 2003. After a tiring series of flights, first from Oregon to Florida and then from Florida to Munich, Germany, our home seemed as an oasis in a dusty world of confusion. It was what we had worked for and dreamed about for a number of years. Once we made the trip down from Munich four hours south to our home, we felt at ease. As we walked through the door, we knew we were home.

Our stop in Florida was made to see my wife's mother Dora and to spend some time with her before departing for Europe. There was a myriad of things that needed doing to *tidy-up* our life in America. We had to leave our car in Oregon with the understanding that it would later be sold by a friend. There were final bills to pay and our house and other property had still not closed escrow. These were nervous days filled with anxiety and worry. The counterbalancing comfort to all of our small confrontations was always the voice of Dora; reassuring in a world that decidedly wasn't. We spent two weeks with Dora before leaving for Italy. During this time, we made preliminary plans with her for a visit to our home in Italy. Although no firm date was set, Dora was looking forward to the trip. As we left her apartment in the airport shuttle, her face seemed worried. We reassured her that we would see each other again soon and off we went into a new world and a new life.

After we arrived in Tret, we immediately set about getting our new life together. Slowly through the coming months, we built our new existence and carefully became a part of our new community. Tret is tiny by any measure with only 278 people as inhabitants. Our arrival made the official population 280 and this in itself was big news for months. We attended church regularly as much for the social contact as for any religion received. Churches in small villages do in fact provide the lifeblood of the community. This is where you receive your news, your dinner invitations and all of the little bits of information that are needed for daily living. We enjoyed our daily excursions into our village and the surrounding communities. Little by little, we became used to our surroundings and a part of the lifeblood of our community.

The planning for Dora's trip started soon after our own arrival as we had so strongly encouraged Dora to come and stay with us a bit and share our enthusiasm for this part of the world. Our first consideration was a bed for our much-loved guest. We spent three months shopping for a guest bed and matching furniture for our small second bedroom. The task proved a bit daunting as furniture is hard to buy in this part of the world. Finally, the exact finishing touches were added and our guest bedroom was ready to receive its first guest.

Almost a year after our arrival in Tret and after much planning for the trip, finally, the long-awaited day arrived and we eagerly drove to Munich to pick-up Rachel's mother. Predictably, the plane was late and then to our horror, mom was not even on the plane when it finally arrived. After a couple of frustrating hours and the rendering of my best German, another plane arrived from Dusseldorf and out at last came Dora. We were relieved to the point of tears and whisked her away from the airport without further delay.

We stopped briefly in Innsbruck on the way back to our home which is located on the south side of the Brenner Pass. Innsbruck is a great pedestrian city and so we stopped for lunch and a quick look at the city square. It was becoming apparent already that long walks would not be Dora's forte on this trip, so we immediately began limiting our excursions as not to entail too much walking. Dora was in good health but eight decades old.

Our home, the Val di Non, is filled with history and a thousand things for the tourist to see and do. We were anxious to share our new life and home with Rachel's mother. There were endless things to see and do in three short weeks and we soon learned that most would have to be overlooked in favor of time. However, there was so much we wanted to share.

The most important part of our new life was the people in our small village. With this in mind, we began to introduce Dora to many of the village's residents and to many of my distant cousins. These fine people of Tret took to Dora immediately and treated her as one of their own. We spent many days at the dining tables of our friends, introducing Dora to the people, the food and the local customs. These visits were punctuated here and there with half-day trips to nearby sights. Dora's visit was going very smoothly and everyone felt a bit blessed by her visit.

Saturday, May 22 came without fanfare and we went about our normal routine. Dora would be with us only a short while longer so we wanted to spend that time at home with her. However, she wanted to see our friend Silvia whom she had met a week or so before. She had purchased a small gift for Silvia and Dora wanted to deliver it in person. We went to Silvia's house and shared a few stories and a bit of tea before proceeding to our house for lunch. Lunch was light and so was the conversation. The day was proceeding as it normally did without a hint of what was to come.

After lunch, we continued talking. I honestly forget the subject. The three of us were seated at our kitchen table. I got up to get a magazine in the living room. When I turned around, Dora was gone. She had died instantly at our table, without warning, without pain. My wife and I knew instantly that we had lost mom in a cruel twist of fate. However, the heart often does not believe the same things as the mind. We struggled with the reality in the first moments and we still continue to struggle with it today.

Everything has a beginning and an end. Our first year was marked by happiness and a sadness so profound that it shall forever escape proper words of description. Our first year was our mother's last year and this true irony is both a benediction of our new life and the blessing of a mother forever loved.

And so Dora, this last chapter is for you. You will forever be loved and will forever be a part of our lives and of our first year. God bless you!

About the Author

Allen E. Rizzi was born in Salt Lake City, Utah, the first child of three born to his parents Barbara Lee Allen and Eugenio Valentino Rizzi. He was raised in Southern California where he studied literature and history. He is a graduate of the California State University at Northridge with a bachelor's degree in English and credentials to teach English and history.

Although English was the only language ever spoken in the Rizzi household throughout his childhood, Allen later learned several other languages including German, Spanish, Italian, French and Latin. He is still struggling with the dialect of his new home, *Nones*. These languages proved to be a beneficial impetus for his later research, studies and writings on the subjects of family heritage, genealogy and the history of the Tirol.

The author has been a professional writer for over 50 years with a diverse background in fiction, non-fiction, poetry, drama, music and short stories. His work has appeared in numerous publications in the United States and in Italy. Additionally, his photographic skills have earned him recognition, along with his wife, in the field of wildlife and travel photography. He is also a published authority on the ancient coinage of Greece, Rome and the Tirol.

His interest in the history of the Tirol began when he was a young man after hearing tales of the "old country" from his father and grandmother. The family's roots in the *Terza Sponda* villages of Cloz and Brez in the Val di Non began to gradually intrigue him. He and his wife Rachel have traveled around the world, including Mexico, Europe and Africa. They made over six trips to Italy and Austria from 1999 to 2002, carefully chronicling the life, history and customs of the South Tirol. Enchanted with the area and its people, the couple decided to move to Italy permanently in 2003. Allen and Rachel have lived in the small village of Tret di Fondo in Italy's Trento Province for over ten years.

Made in United States
North Haven, CT
28 November 2021

11624543R10093